BOOK WORMS

Ready for School
We Are Kind

Listos para ir a la escuela
Somos amables

Sharon Gordon

Marshall Cavendish
Benchmark
New York

We are kind.

Somos amables.

3

We help others.
We are kind.

❖

Ayudamos a los demás.

Somos amables.

We teach them.
We are kind.

—————◆—————

Les enseñamos.
Somos amables.

We share.
We are kind.

❖

Compartimos.
Somos amables.

We work together.
We are kind.

Trabajamos juntos.
Somos amables.

We play together.
We are kind.

Jugamos juntos.
Somos amables.

We care for pets.

We are kind.

Cuidamos a las mascotas.

Somos amables.

We give hugs.
We are kind.

———————❖———————

Nos abrazamos.
Somos amables.

We say thank-you.
We are kind!

Decimos gracias.
¡Somos amables!

19

We Are Kind

Somos amables

care
cuidar

help
ayudar

hug
abrazar

play
jugar

share
compartir

teach
enseñar

thank-you
gracias

work
trabajar

21

Index

Índice

About the Author
Datos biográficos de la autora

Sharon Gordon has written many books for young children. She has always worked as an editor. Sharon and her husband Bruce have three children, Douglas, Katie, and Laura, and one spoiled pooch, Samantha. They live in Midland Park, New Jersey.

Sharon Gordon ha escrito muchos libros para niños. Siempre ha trabajado como editora. Sharon y su esposo Bruce tienen tres niños, Douglas, Katie y Laura, y una perra consentida, Samantha. Viven en Midland Park, Nueva Jersey.

With thanks to Nanci Vargus, Ed.D. and
Beth Walker Gambro, reading consultants

Marshall Cavendish Benchmark
99 White Plains Road
Tarrytown, New York 10591-9001
www.marshallcavendish.us

Library of Congress Cataloging-in-Publication Data

Gordon, Sharon.
We are kind = Somos amables / Sharon Gordon. — Bilingual ed.
p. cm. — (Bookworms, ready for school = Listos para ir a la escuela)
Includes index.
ISBN-13: 978-0-7614-2435-2 (bilingual edition)
ISBN-10: 0-7614-2435-0 (bilingual edition)
ISBN-13: 978-0-7614-2356-0 (Spanish edition)
ISBN-10: 0-7614-1992-6 (English edition)
1. Kindness—Juvenile literature. I. Title. II. Title: Somos amables.

BJ1533.K5G67 2006
177'.7—dc22
2006018213

Spanish Translation and Text Composition by Victory Productions, Inc.
www.victoryprd.com

Photo Research by Anne Burns Images

Cover by *Corbis*/Blane Harrington III

The photographs in this book are used with permission and through the courtesy of:
Corbis: pp. 1, 17, 20 (bottom l) Owen Franken; p. 3 Tom & Dee Ann McCarthy; pp. 7, 19, 21 (top r),
21 (bottom l) Royalty Free; pp. 9, 21 (top l) Ted Horowitz; p. 13, 20 (bottom r) Ariel Skelley;
pp. 15, 20 (top l) Hutchings Stock Photography. *SuperStock*: pp. 5, 11, 20 (top r), 21 (bottom r) AGE Fotostock.

Printed in Malaysia
1 3 5 6 4 2